More Titles Available by John Golden
Roaming Lions Press

A Tear From A Glass Eye (2010)

Sons of the Silent Age (2010)

The Dying Tree (2010)

Dead Sky, Pale Lights (2010)

The 75 Club (2011)

The Dying Tree

John Golden

The Dying Tree edited by Michele Golden & Dennis Zanabria.
Cover art by Monica Magana.

ISBN 978-0-615-40415-8

USA $18.00 / CAN $20.00

First Roaming Lions Press Edition

For Michele, your patience and love breed creativity.

Author's Introduction

For far too long we have been stationary, much like trees. We have stopped feeding our minds with arcane knowledge. We have lost our spirituality to greed and "The American Dream."

The concept for *The Dying Tree* came out of my desire to make people care again. As humans we need to feel and realize that humanity is not just a forgotten word. As humans we cannot remain stationary to the suffering of others and to the state of our world. We remain happy within the confines of our routine schedules. Day after day it's the same old thing. We go to work and come home. We go through our evening rituals only to start again with the rising sun of each new day. All the while there is an entire world around us that we rarely think about. As long as our daily schedules are not disrupted we seem to be content. This all must stop. We have to pull our head out of the charcoal fog and look at the bigger picture. Although it is often uncomfortable to remove the blindfold from our eyes to outside problems and restart the wheels of rational thinking, it is what each and every one of us must do if we truly want to change our world for the better.

Trees are majestic and need nutrients to live. We are not so different. If we don't fill ourselves up with things that feed the intellect and make us aware on a grander scale we will surely die-spirit, soul, mind and body. We become dying trees devoid of spirituality and compassion. Wake up! Breathe! Feel again! Dare to be human again! As I've said before, our inheritance is this world to change for the better or the worse. It is truly up to us. I hope you enjoy this collection of poems. More importantly, I hope my work will inspire you in some way or another to do better. We can all be better people. Cut the noose and come down from the dying tree.

Cheers and happy reading!

John Golden
June 6, 2010

The Dying

T
R
E
E

John Golden

Roaming Lions Press 2010

I
Broken Branches & Crooked Crosses
Crippled branch arches now passing the dead world.

Long Beach After Midnight

There's inspiration in strange things
Take refuge in the night
Shadows and dust
There's inspiration in strange things
A chipped wooden table
Shopping cart heroes roaming Los Angeles
There's inspiration in strange things
Take refuge in the night

The Eternal Affair

I'm in love with everyone
This seems to be a problem
Women don't like to share
I'm in love with everyone
I'm addicted to life and
Emotion that burns like gasoline on a skeleton
I'm in love with everyone
This seems to be a problem

Everyone's a Colleague

Sarcasm is a bitter pill
Most people annoy me
With their petty bullshit
Sarcasm is a bitter pill
Frog faced people
So quick to judge
Sarcasm is a bitter pill
Most people annoy me

2nd Street Circa 2003

Slip into a black abyss
Night, it slowly crawls
Candlestick fingers dripping sweet wine
Slip into a black abyss
And I will surely submit to it
Every time it calls
Slip into a black abyss
Night, it slowly crawls

Charlotte's Domain

My web is not tangled
Like everyone else's
My sincerity is not controlled by a clock
My web is not tangled
No time clock death card
Has a hold on my bearings
My web is not tangled
Like everyone else's

Ode

He's not here anymore
Drunken heroes fall
He's not here anymore
Stolen youth lies on the deck of a ship
He's not here anymore
Tackle box doctors
Emptying souls on a floor
He's not here anymore
Drunken heroes fall

Screw Ferris

Everybody loves him
Ferris Bueller was a jerk
Manipulative little son of a bitch
Everybody loves him
I see right through your selfish intentions
Fucking over everyone you know for your own benefit
Everybody loves him
Ferris Bueller was a jerk

Rotten Apples

Tell the doctor I'll be late
I've got better things to do
Than wait for his death sentence
Tell the doctor I'll be late
I'll treat the homeless man to a smile and a meal
I'll help an orphan find a home
Tell the doctor I'll be late
I've got better things to do

Cougar

Your lust becomes you
Dripping sweet perfume and death on the floor
I'll be your secret sin for awhile
Your lust becomes you
Ugly mirror monster
Corroded by time and insecurity
Your lust becomes you
Dripping sweet perfume and death on the floor

Highway Morality

Jesus is handcuffed to every bumper in America
Staring us straight in the eye
Begging for a release
Jesus is handcuffed to every bumper in America
Screaming to be peeled off from
Metallic rolling death coffins
Jesus is handcuffed to every bumper in America
Staring us straight in the eye

Stimulant

Black coffee spiders
Crawling on my floor
It's happening again
Black coffee spiders
With transparent tape recorders
Taking snapshots of my mind
Black coffee spiders
Crawling on my floor

3 A.M. Standing Naked

Yesterday's tears
Paint an ambient skyline
Across her once sculpted face
Yesterday's tears
Serve as a constant reminder
That an empty bed is cold
Yesterday's tears
Paint an ambient skyline

Station 407

I'll make my escape
On this lonely train tonight
Small town blues got me ramblin'
I'll make my escape
In faded denim freedom
That holds all I own
I'll make my escape
On this lonely train tonight

Butterfingers

Don't let the good ones slip away
It's rare that they come around
Perhaps even more rare that we realize it
Don't let the good ones slip away
Like empty bottles hitting pavement
Broken pieces cannot be put back together
Don't let the good ones slip away
It's rare that they come around

Walking Dead

The wolves have been let out
Better watch your back little one
Roaming desolate alleys
The wolves have been let out
Inhaling moonlight and dreams
Prowling for flesh and souls
The wolves have been let out
Better watch your back little one

D.C. Dilemma

Don't drink the water
It will not suffice
The deep thirst of a lost love
Don't drink the water
Exhausted emery boards and
Empty tan pill bottles wash down regret
Don't drink the water
It will not suffice

Flight 227

I really don't need this memory
I should have scalped my ticket
Uncle Jack screwed me again
I really don't need this memory
Or the scent of your auburn hair
As you bent down from the passenger seat
I really don't need this memory
I should have scalped my ticket

Right to Die Blues

Take this old soul
And shine it like a rusted steel can
Make me whole again
Take this old soul
And stamp a name on it
America's gone and forgotten me
Take this old soul
And shine it like a rusted steel can

Joy in Death

They're not here anymore
To experience this
Senseless tears of remorse
They're not here anymore
Stuck helpless on a freeway
Starving for an idea, waiting for a prayer
They're not here anymore
To experience this

Twinkie Defense

We've all heard the story
About the health nut who
Gets hit by a car while jogging,
Or the vegan who develops
Cancer, or how about the
Vegetarian who gets mauled
By a bear?

We all strive for health
While Jared masturbates
Into a chalupa of shame
And teenage girls stand
Before an accusing mirror
Trying to live up to a bullshit
Plastic American ideal of beauty.

Alcohol is bad, but
Wine is good for your heart.
Fucked up food pyramid
Of hypocrisy says to
Get your daily serving
Of bread, cereal, rice and pasta
Even though it all
Turns to sugar in the end.

I shouldn't smoke,
But it's perfectly
Acceptable to drive through
Smog filled Los Angeles
With the windows down
While stuck in traffic
Behind a bus belching smoke
Like a concrete whale.

I can legally drink until the point
Where I'm loaded and ready to drive
Home endangering all around me,

But God forbid I smoke
A joint on my couch
And pass out with a
Plate full of half-eaten nachos in my lap.

Enemas, cholesterol,
Injections and doctor's halls
It's enough to make
My skin crawl.

Optimal health defined
By the standards of others,
Uncle Sam has on
His apron ready to
Feed us all
Provided we have a home.
It's a whole different
Story if you're homeless,
A whole different poem
For that matter.

Body image doesn't define
A free mind and tons
Of perfectly healthy
People die every day.
In the end, when
Your numbers up
You're finished
So why the hell should
I think about the
Sweet salvation that
I cram into my
Mouth and lungs everyday…
Nobody ever orders a salad
For a last meal.

Happy Hour

Come all ye embittered
Corporate slaves and
Gather round the table.
Drink the sweet
Nectar of forgetfulness
And regret as you
Spill your sorrows
To your jaded co-workers
Who will soon stab you
In the back, much
Like the plastic sword
That pierces the olive
In your martini.

Hell is Lonesome (Too Many People Like Me)

I have seen hell,
I have walked brave
And blind among
Its obscure rails
Yelling and slurring obscenities
To its unhappy residents.

I've pissed on its floors,
Thrown up in its black basalt bathrooms.
I've fought its untamed beasts
And philosophized with opulent harlots.
I've witnessed the massacre
Of my submerged mind.

Drunkenly doomed as Oedipus,
I've bred chaos and
Seen the invention of the bottle.
Futile attempts at happiness
Swallowed in dark secret corners.
Spiritual bankruptcy signed
On a yellow slip of paper.

Yes, I've been to hell
Far too many times
And I can tell you this much,
You don't need a passport,
Your ID will suffice.

Downtown Delirium

Blood roses for apologies
Of an inebriated night
Wandering floors searching
For happiness while
Sympathetic elevator boys
Take my drunken gratuities
Leading me through cobweb
Passages with mascara clad
Goblins pouring cocaine
On my soul, my eyes
Becoming blurred saltshakers
Pouring liar's dust into my
Sweet surrender that
She may hear one last time.

Organ Thieves and Liver Spots

I've never seen intellect
And dollars matched up too well,
Much like politicians and integrity.
The tiger that was once sober
Is now drunk, his mismatched stripes arranged
On a canvas of fear and doubt.
Numbers and statistics
Make liars out of orators
And fools of those
Willing to believe.

There is a great depth to humans
If allowed to express their
Individuality without concern
Of being judged by pompous
Self-appointed sages
Who feast on money and power.
It's time to strike
Down the elitist mentality
And rise as a collective
Force of free thinking
Individuals hell-bent
On intellectual revolution
And self-expression.

Sin City Salutation

The illuminated counterculture
Of Las Vegas creates
A visible pulse in the night
Where hunchbacked dinosaurs
Put coins into belching
Electric circus machines.

Intoxicated soldiers in
Their huddled masses
Wearing bone white togas
Gardening for an easy hustle
And loose lipped harlots
In this neon empire of debauchery.

There's never a full moon
In this graveyard desert
Of an oasis for those
Chain-smoking blue hairs
And the ample breasted
Ladies with red lace
Brassieres to hold up
Styrofoam breasts as
Hollow as the sharks in
Suits coming over the horizon.

The townsfolk have been
Replaced by vampires
And dried-up cinematic angels
Marble orchards in bloom
Among flashing lights and
Slurred syllables eaten
By smoke rings and spring
Colored taxicabs with
Pictures of semi-naked
Death women for sale.

Everyone's soul dies

A little with each
Visit where epic tales
Of postmodern excitement
And conceptual freedom
Paint a picture of inhumanity.

The tide of booze, blood
And cigarette butts is
Rising as a lucky few
Grab their vests and
Jump into their steel caged
Lifeboats that dart
Drearily down the I-15.

The Other Side of Seuss

Fart for art
Art is fart
Fart on darts
Dart on farts
Parts of farts
Sting like darts
Carts of darts
Dipped in farts
All for art
And broken hearts

Who says Dr. Seuss is dead?

Milestones

Candy for breakfast
Is what the children want
The teenager wants the
Keys to the car
For a first taste of freedom
The college student
Wants money for books
That he will soon sell for beer.

The homeless want compassion
To justify their sorrows
The adult wants to understand
Why he can't buy peace
With money
The old man contemplates
His life wondering if
He did right with his time
The hitchhiker looks at life
Through a borrowed
Rear view mirror.

So many wants and desires
Keeping us from our dreams
Intruding upon our egos
As we quietly wither
Away under an unforgiving
Sun that will rise as surely
As it sets
Just as it has from the
Day of time's creation.

We spin lost memories
On a highway toward
Death and decay
A subtle reminder
Of a far away ticking
That will surely go on

Just as it has from
The day of time's creation.

The Blasé Burglar

Casually elegant scavengers
Escaping through hidden windows
Concealed behind garages and
Potted plants, driving stolen
Mercedes full of nylon roses
And other senseless treasures
Snatched from weeping doors.

Walk of Fame

Love strands hanging from
Her matted hair
Quivering guilt burning
Through the faint flicker
Of moonlight that spells
Out harlot across her
Broad rounded shoulders.

My loose lizard tongue
Tries to give her
A parting farewell,
But words are lost
Among carbon copy
Apologies that carry
As much weight
As the evening's lost promises.

Buk's Concern

Bukowski had a secret bluebird
He kept hidden from society.
If that varmint ever escaped
All of the "cocks" and "fucks"
Would turn to meaningless trite.

Morrison probably had a bluebird too
Nestled deep within the
Soul of a sad clown.
Had that one gotten away
The poor intoxicated bastard
Probably would have flown into a wall.

I have quite the opposite affliction,
I keep a demon inside
Though mine isn't such
A secret, just feed
Him some Jack Daniels
And that little fucker
Will tell you my life story.

Late Shift

Light bulb stoplights and
Candlelight turn-offs,
The pulse of the tidal freeway
Slows a bit after midnight.
Retired off-ramp vendors
Pushing shopping carts of plunder
Into thickets of empty eternity.
Discarded bottles of wine
And orange trash bags
Pave the way home
As Miles blares
Through my speakers,
Some kind of blue indeed.

Sparrows and Swans

Blue silent stars
Together in a flowered field
Fog streams down over
Bare calves and jeweled feet
Poetic illuminations blowing
Smoke into the invulnerable night
As we dance among rare
Wild beasts, piano key
Fingers hold my heavy
Neck as we kiss
Under a canopy of paradise
As naked as the night
Without its long black veil.

Ghostwind Landscapes

Savor the night
And its clairvoyant stars
Great guardian of the
Poets and wanderers
Crouched under cobwebbed constellations.

Savor the night,
Its moonlit shrouds
Feed the starving
Mind of the poet
With stardust spoons.

The incandescent moon
Guards celestial resurrections,
Dazzling ghostwind landscapes
For the philosophers and junkies.

Cool fog-harrowed hills,
Branches dancing triumphantly
In the gentle mist,
Lantern lit lullabies
Lure me toward
The monument of
God's great nocturnal design.

Incense fountains nourishing
Shapeless shadows flung
In nightly orbit under
A tipping cloud candelabra.

Angel Gabriel Hates San Gabriel

Dusty vaqueros on horses
Greet the highway
Roaming what little
Of nature is left
In the coarse San Gabriel Valley.

Bubblegum umbrellas shade
Vendors selling fruit on
This small stretch of
Highway that time seems
To have misplaced.
A quarter mile ahead
I'm greeted by a traffic
Light that makes a bold
Statement that progress
Always steals what's
Left of nature and ancient landscapes.

Wisdom Through Age and Pain

The commitment of distrust
Takes many years to master,
Countless heartbreaks and letdowns
Mind fucked into insanity and doubt
Infecting like poison
Clawing at reason.
The manipulators, the liars
We have all worked hard
At our craft which
Takes another bite
Out of the human condition.

Bastards and beggars searching
For a reason to believe in
Anything, only to find
A shell-shocked discontent
In the realization that
We are all slowly
Dying for humanity's sins
Stained by every cruel
Word and insincerity
Carved into our subconscious.

II
Waking the Wounded
Hope is no stocking stuffer

Written in the Dark

TV shadows burning chaos through a screen
Incoherent spheres of fiber
Optics bringing in massive
Amounts of disaster into homes,
A new and furious education
For the youth of America.

Naked skin mutated actresses
And Twitter tombstones
Homeschool the children
In this unimaginable
Melancholy age of media.

Diamond spinners and firewalls
Texting Zen to a generation
Of indifference whose
Downloading dirges have
Killed the recording industry.

No turning back from
The dark courses of technology,
There are no jewels
To be found within the click
Of a mouse, only the
Blind led into an
Ocean of useless information
One pixel at a time.

PCH Waitress

Sleeved waitress in a black shirt
With earplugs and a look of
Partially hidden distress.
I wonder if she secretly dreams
Of Rock 'n' Roll fortune while
Waiting these scuffed lacquered tables.

Another night of wishing she
Was somewhere else among
Anarchy, amps and tattooed angels.
Hollywood is a long way from
Long Beach when you've worked
The graveyard shift and all
Of the bands have left the stage.
The parties have dissipated,
Groupies passed out, musicians
Searching for loose change between
Ripped stained sofas hoping to
Find enough money to cop a
Sack of dope.

Somehow she misses this,
She longs for this environment
Of chaotic killers with crudely painted faces.
You can see the sadness in her eyes.
Frustration slowly birthing tears
Behind an emotionless steel register.
If she only knew
How safe she is in this café
Sanctuary of careless eaters
And bad tippers.
There's a part of me that wants
To reach out to her
To scream, "Stay here!
Don't go out into the wild Los Angeles
Night! Don't let them destroy
You! Rebuild your dreams on

Wings of sanity and fly free."

Anniversary

Mountains bow down to her ageless beauty
Confusion falls over those she walks past
Grand birds suspended in flight
Each word she speaks escaped and frozen
Shaking hands fly up to grab each precious syllable.

In all the world
Even in its most remote corners
Even in the light of a spring day
Or under the tranquil quiet of a setting moon
There is nothing as beautiful as her
And I have the ring to prove it.

Late Nite Supper

Milk in chipped glasses
Chili served from steel pots
Deep fried depression of cooks
Who long for citizenship
Crying children with embarrassed parents
Drunk college kids spewing nonsense
Plastic marlin on the wall
Overhearing everything
Hapless lovers trying to patch things up
All of this going on
As I wait for my dinner.

A Most Solitary Street

Black tar outlining manholes on
The street with a fragile line
Connecting the two,
T.J. Eckleburg has fallen.
The eyes of God
Now watch from below
As careless tires roll past
And smoldering cigarette butts
Fly out of radiant cars,
Their falling embers
Ignite the death of America.

Thanks to Ken

No need to visit
Japan and its grand landscapes,
Rexroth already showed me
More of Japan and its
Illustrious offerings than
I could see in one hundred trips.

Far Too Subtle

Dropping plastic glasses
Doesn't have the same effect
As the dramatic sound of breaking glass
Dropping plastic glasses
Doesn't have the anger and rage
That a bloody hand smashing glass has
Dropping plastic glasses
Doesn't have the same effect

Diplomatic Immunity

I do believe that Santa
Is the only man in the world
Who can stroll into any
Mall in America and
Charge children money
To sit in his lap
And reveal their innermost secrets
Without getting arrested.

Trespassing

Chewing gum thoughts
Glued to the pavement,
Secret memories of
Strangers passing by
As cars hiss along in
A metallic death line.

It makes me sad to
Gaze upon this notebook
Sidewalk trying to decipher
People's discarded ideas
That so many carelessly step on.

Airline Enlightenment

Farting on an airplane
Is like sharing your
Innermost secrets with
A bunch of strangers,
The only difference is
That now I have a
Captive audience to
Listen to my crap.

One of the Crowd

Conversing in the checkout
Line as an old lady
Waits for the bag boy
To bring her Marlboros,
Magazine racks tell
Of shamed celebrities,
A whiny kid throws
Candy into his mother's
Cart in a last attempt
At independence.
All of this going
On while I patiently
Wait for a book of stamps.

Nothing more than a letter
Waiting to be sent to a
Long lost friend who
Moved out of the city
To get away from
Such informal gatherings.

Lullabies of the Deceased

Crystal hymns diffused beneath
Black railroad tracks
Bitter musical secrets
Shared by the dead
Banished forever by
Kaleidoscope gypsies who
Camp on packed street corners.

Such pretty songs
Generously handed down
To religion and paranoid
Sociopaths who are soothed
By their witchery.

Who will deny the corpse
His dying rights of melody?
The hectic streets of life
Pulse with your rhythms
Mesmerizing romantics
And urban scarecrows.

Reincarnated arias pushed
Casually through hermits' lips
In tiny forgotten window ledge towns.
Champagne shadows hum your
Tunes through lonely restaurants
Where stale cigarettes and vintage scotch
Carry your tormented melodies
Into a misty midnight orbit.

A cavalry of dancers
On gravestones
Bursting into a tornado chorus
That is sung and known by all.

Hold Your Applause (It's Not What You're Thinking)

Reading *The Catcher in the Rye*
Was amazing when I was in high school.
Holden was a rebel, he said
Goddamn and crap, and chain-smoked
Like a locomotive.
He ditched school, drank
And picked up hookers.
He was a fucking rock star
When I was fifteen.

Teaching Salinger's supposed
Masterpiece in my mid-thirties
Is a different story.
Holden was the biggest
Phony in the book.
He was nothing more than
A spoiled rich kid,
Insecure and lacking friends.
A guy that swears like a
Sailor but then turns
Around and erases *fuck* off of walls.
A hypocrite in every sense of the word.

I wonder now if he was a pedophile
With his obsessive interest in his sister Phoebe.
I reread over one hundred pages listening to this
Whiny red headed freckled faced fuck.
This selfish prick who spent more
Time worrying about himself than
The thousands of dollars his
Parents had flushed down
The toilet for countless
Private schools that he flunked out of.

I now realize that he never
Banged that hooker, my teenage
Mind had created a myth just

As so many others who still
See him as a savior protecting
Children from the evils of
The world.
Do any of you
Realize that your myths
You've created loaded the
Gun that killed Lennon and
Shot Reagan?
You've kept him
Frozen in your adolescent
Minds, not seeing truth,
Not willing to accept reality,
Just like Holden.

Pencey Prep, Ackely Kid, "Sleep
Tight Ya Morons." You immortalize
This snot-nosed shit who thought
He was better than everyone else.
This arrogant frightened
Child who couldn't hold his
Liquor or face his parents
Is a hero in your eyes.
This kid whose epic piece
Of writing consisted of
An essay about his dead brother's
Baseball mitt.

Can't you see that he was
Just another person who
Couldn't deal with death,
Who lamented the loss of
His brother,
Who wondered where
The ducks in Central
Park went in the winter
When the pond froze over?

I can answer that question

That the cab driver so
Rudely refused to answer.
The ducks leave because
They realize the solitary truth
That they must grow up.
They must move on to evolve,
To experience life, because
Even animals know that to
Judge is wrong, that wings must
Spread in order to flourish.

They know better than most
That wandering around a city
Self-absorbed and wounded
Is to spiritually die,
So they fly free because they
Can't be caught
With the winds
They solely own.

Thick Skin

Insults are like
Sawdust cannonballs
That drop like wingless birds
In the face of logic.

Force Feeding Mother Earth

Charcoal horizon smears the earth
And paves the compressed asphalt.
Lubricated mountains covered in soot,
Anonymous death warrant signed
By piggy bank corporations and crudely
Served to Mother Earth.

Sundance knives and leather characters
Swaggering together unmasking shadows
Pillaging oil, draining the electricity
Out of reading lights until
There are no words or
Wisdom at all.
These are the faded images
Of a notebook world bought
And sold into extinction.

Open Mic (Five Minutes of Fame)

Nothing worse than
An answer back audience
With papers sticking out
Of pen smeared folders.
The next self-proclaimed
Ferlinghetti gets his five
Minutes or three poems.
Clapping out of obligation
For accepted mediocrity.
Shaking hand silence,
Thick cheeks blotting out words,
Clanking cups, buzzing phones
On vibrate.

Wolf shirts and wolf poems,
A terrible *Howl*.
An occasional talent,
Mostly retirees and rehab rejects.
It's a good crowd,
You just gotta listen to
A few of them.

Lady Lights

Mountains exist behind cold
Steel illusions and tagged up
Freeway signs.
Birds fly above scarred red
Sunsets of abstract fog
Beauty.
Married to the whore I love,
The city of Los Angeles.

Stillwater

The uneasy dead
Accompany me while
I dream of drifting
Fishing boats singing
Softly and dancing
In the fragile breeze.

Painted faces vanish
In the fog of
An autumn evening
That feels like Halloween.

Emotional Trend

Twilight derelict
Skull white vampire children
Stepping out of the cinema
Looking for a chiseled champion.
Emotionally confused teens
Acting crazy on purpose,
A disturbing new American fad.

Take thy blade and cut
Deep into the flesh.
Cut out all of the
Devil's profit you've been
Force-fed through
Bruised movie screens.
Bleed out the phoniness
And spiked hair honeymoon hunchbacks.
Leave them all behind
Step into the daylight
And figure out how to be
A real person.

Gridlock in Armageddon

Dark demonic hashish shadows,
Sunset fishermen astounded
As reporters roll in to
Capture camouflage con men
All attempting to kiss
Crucifixes in shrouds
As crumbling coffin scriptures
Pour from contradicting tongues.

Our world ravaged in a day.
Wailing galleries of chaos,
Wild-haired banshees
Float among the
Cloudless Western sky.
The freeway at a
Dead halt with people
Exiting cars to witness
The fantastic end
Of our debauched universe.

It's times such as these
That I'm glad I carry
A cooler in my car,
Whiskey whirlwinds come
On down, I'm going out
With a solid buzz.

III
Memento Mori

The dead bell rings as the angels stand aside

Death (The Grand Coda)

Death, I've given you almost
  as much as you've taken.
  My first child at seventeen,
  my panic attacks,
  my drunken binges and broken crucifixes.
Death, I used to hide under cowboy
  blankets frightened at night.
Death, you invade my midnight dreams.
  I'm obsessed by your coffins,
  ancient cemeteries, and shadow galleries.
  Fuck you Death, take off your
  cloak and fight like a man.
  Show your hollow face
  that I read about every
  day in the LA Times.
  Stop slinking around like a
  kid in a candy store.
Death, your prostitutes
  smell of your loathsome stench.
  My therapist thinks we should
  break up,
  but I know the truth,
  you can't live without me.
Death, your home on Wall Street
  serves you well riding your pale horse
  down Broadway.
Death, you've constructed your armies of Armageddon.
  Your soldiers work hard for you
  destroying what took centuries to build
  and seconds to disappear.
Death, you're an ungrateful prick.
  You're a fucking coward
  sucker punching people
  when they least expect it.
  Movie producers turn out your
  precious zirconium starlets,
  the same ones you peddle dope to.

Death, I've drank your concoctions
        and ruined countless lives.
        Your money wrecks families
        and destroys dreams.
        I give birth to you
        every time I cry.
Death, do you think my suicide
        notes are love letters?
        Is my anger a warm embrace
        to you?
Death, you have no lips for the
        widow to kiss.
Death, you ship slaves,
        make addicts and ban gay marriage.
        I read your billboards of
        false prophecy and bathe
        in your pools of acid rain.
        You've made an addict out
        of me and a nation
        of voyeurs glued to a
        television screen of disaster.
        You're the scab I keep picking
        never to heal like my eyes, open wounds.
        You're the carbonized footprint I leave.
Death, you don't really
        want people to die.
        You want us to live in
        fear and distrust.
        You're a homophobe, a rapist,
        a loan shark, a broken hearted seraphim.
Death, your ugly little secret
        I'll tell the world,
        you're as afraid as we are.
        I'll reconstruct your churches of madness
        and sacrifice you on an altar of love.
        I'll take back the dreams
        that are rightfully mine.
        I'll stitch up your wounds
        one person at a time.

Death, I'm turning my back
        on you and your tombstone temples.
Death, I'll put skin back on
        your naked skeletons.
        I will not be
        your embarrassed ambassador assassin.
        No longer will you use my tongue to
        taunt those you can't
        reach.
Death, I'll free your slaves
        and disarm your countries.
Death, bow down to your god;
        I wear his face.
        I ride on your blacktop cloak roads.
        I blow out your cigarette
        birthday candles and extinguish
        your existence.
Death, you can take back your Xanax
        and sharp silver tall cans.
        I've unwrapped your mummies
        and they've spoke of you.
        You only have power over life.
Death, you have no home to
        go to in eternity.
        My soul will not be your garage,
        my paranoia will not be your excuse,
        my children will not be your followers.
Death, your pupils have failed you:
        Hitler, Judas, Pol Pot, Vlad,
        Caligula, Manson, Nero, and Cain.
        Heaven has beaten your body count.
Death, you chew crucifixes like
        sunflower seeds.
        You built the Vatican out of
        catacomb bones.
        Your cynical laughter haunts me.
Death, you stand out at a masquerade
        without even wearing a mask.
Death, your gifts are free.

Your bank account soars by
    every soul sold.
Death, your gift wrap is made from flesh,
    no wonder I'm crying.
Death, waiting for you is like
    the bus home that never comes.
Death, your crosses hang upside down
    giving company to Saint Peter.
Death, continue as a phantom,
    give up the ghost already.
Death, you have parking stalls at every
    hotel, hospital and hostel.
Death, the harm that you cause will
    become your own.
Death, America supplies
    you with your cyanide vitamins.
Death, you're nothing more
    than a magic trick.
Death, you act like you've never had love.
Death, your soldiers pray to you
    instead of God.
Death, you never said goodnight to Poe
    but he knew your name
    drunkenly calling out,
    "Reynolds, Reynolds, Reynolds"
    as he tasted his last bit of rain
    in the Baltimore gutter
    patiently awaiting your arrival.
Death, I watch you happily dance with
    the newly dead at your cemeteries.
Death, tell Dillinger not to fall in love
    anymore.
Death, you begin your letters
    with *"Dear Victims..."*
Death, you swallow the American eagle
    and crap out bats.
Death, Howard Hughes went crazy
    trying to find you.
Death, you own all of America and her

saltwater tears and her marched down mountains
and raped her
prairie landscapes and sent Whitman
early to the grave.
Death, you're waiting in line
like the rest of us.
Does your touch seduce the young?
Do your footprints scorch the
farmers' fields?
Death, you go by many names:
Delilah, Moloch, Abaddon, and Oppenheimer.
Death, your heart is rotting.
Do you dream as I do?
Can you see in colors?
I've seen you con your way
into the justice system
tipping scales with your
skeletal hands of budding corruption.
I've seen your shell-shocked
children from society wander
hollow and nameless.
Death, I've seen your
smile in the newscaster's
face as he reports another tragedy
continuing your legacy.
Your acrid breath reeks
throughout every hospital corridor.
I've seen your cold and calculating
hand control the knife of the surgeon.
I've seen innocent animals
killed by your oil spills
and trusting children lured
into your sinister vans.
Death, you're a grand liar,
an illusion of terror
born out of a frightened child's closet.
You're the bastard child of an
aborted birth, a solitary
shadow clinging onto walls

and infamy as you travel
through our streets of innocence.
Death, you take without asking.
    Your newspapers write your obituaries,
    your authority convicts the innocent
    and frees the corrupt.
Death, I've seen your
    napalm char the motherless child.
    I've witnessed your lackeys
    in high-rise buildings
    take from the working class,
    well-trained thieves disguised
    as accountants, loan brokers,
    and Meyer Wolfsheims.
Death, your greatest accomplishments
    shovel the dirt in the graves
    of our loved ones.
    You're a chickenshit escape artist.
Death, you're a lustful joy
    ripe for the picking
    and this farmer now holds
    the scythe.
Death, I've seen your face
    in the mushroom cloud.
    You burnt out Gatsby's green light.
    You eat the flowers after the funeral.
Death, I can't help but find no
    man here of your design-
    complications of this American mind.
Death, your welcome parties are funerals
    with bastard bagpipes
    playing your unholy hymns.
Death, we talk about you all the time,
    when will you visit?
    You collect our corpses and
    eat our ash and belch it
    out of cold industrial towers.
Death, only once you were kind,
    helping the Elephant Man

build his popsicle stick church.

Death, you deformed Lord Byron's
    leg on purpose, leaving an
    imperfect Adonis.

Death, everyday is your birthday
    celebrated on the front page
    of journals, magazines, newspapers,
    advertisements, and sawdust streetwalkers
    soliciting your gifts.

Death, do you remember
    your brother, Hypnos?

Death, stop stocking your missiles in Cuba,
    Russia, China and North Korea.

Death, you paint the human face
    with pallor mortis.

Death, I will not deify you,
    I will not lionize you,
    I will not promote your hearses in my parades.

Death, you tune your guitars with Heretic's fork.

Death, your spirit I inhale
    and exhale into a barren midnight sky.
    You who invented The American Dream
    that devoured Willy Loman.
    You constructed the house of insanity
    that Sarah Winchester could not finish.

Death, we drink to you every time we clank
    our glasses in counterfeit celebrations.
    Death,
        Death,
            Death,

You're nothing more than a memory passed
    down from a vivid American nightmare.

Death, who is next in line
    to inherit your robe and collect your skulls?

Only the next fool willing to believe your fairytale lie.

Death, to hell with you,
    bring on the death of the American dream.
    I quit.

Youth and Eternity
(Prologue to The Death of the American Dream)

Small town mongrels
Driving cars with smashed fenders
Along the same roads they've
Known since they were
Thin golden haired kids
Dreaming of business suits
And million dollar jobs with uptown apartments
On the Upper East Side of New York City.

Years later these same kids
Who never traveled
Or went barreling through
Towns in corporate limousines
Are spending their afternoons
In the local bars disillusioned
With books, music, life and
Once promising aspirations.

Drifting in helpless shame,
Lone nights spent dreaming about
Lost jobs and wasted love.
The recognition of a brilliant
Future met only in
Tension filled nightmares.

What is left to inherit
For this train wreck generation
Who never made it out
Of sleepy towns?
Only a bitter nostalgia
Of the injured American Dream.

Working Girl
(The Death of the American Dream Part I)

The secretary fondles a
Cigarette between her
Rouge lips, making a sweet
Face while answering phones.
A botched attempt at
Acting civil toward the stone
Voices on the other end of the line.

She dreams of falling asleep
On soft pillows with a boyfriend
Lying down on her bed.
But the sad truth remains
That there is no bluebird
Perched in a tree this morning.

She made the choice years
Ago to put her head in
The mouth of the lion
Marching into the dark
Horizons of the corporate world,
Trading in the rainbows of
Her youth for strange uniforms
And a battle-worn briefcase
That now looks unfamiliar and foreign
With her name imprinted on the
Cracked leather and ideals
And aspirations from a time
That now haunts her with
Its dusky promises that
Anything was possible.

Now forty years later
The aristocrats are still
Meeting across white marble
Tables, middle-aged men blind
To her smiles and compulsive dreams.

She remains a dying warrior
Sitting behind a receptionist's
Desk covered with pictures of
False destinations and green
Plastic plants.
Fighting a war that was won long
Ago by corporate wolves
In iron pressed suits.

She looks down at her nicotine
Stained fingers, very capable hands
Capable of a lot more than she's
Been doing as the gray
Years have inched by.
Somehow the rungs on
The corporate ladder
Dissolved before she
Had a chance to scale
Them into a green sky
Of distinguished security.

She has furiously realized
The truth hidden somewhere
In the back of her mind
That to many, woman are
Not so important.

Dusk disappears into night
Night disappears into day
And another recycled year
Of hope marching over a
Shattered horizon and
Lost opportunities heard
Through hollow trumpets
That belch out dust and depression.

She leaves the familiar office
Saying goodbye to nobody in particular
Hands clasped on her leased BMW

That holds her heavy valise and
Hushed tears of frustration.

Looking straight ahead she
Drives down a nondescript street
Realizing that she is not
Capable of saying goodbye
To children who never
Were conceived through counterfeit lovers,
Saying goodbye to that villa
In France, saying goodbye
To her imaginary cardboard
Articulate husband who
Never seemed to materialize
Into flesh.

She rolls down the window
And lights a cigarette
As the blue flame dances
Among her graying hair
Blown back by the wind.

Saying goodbye is never
Easy, though working
Among rubber potted plants
And faceless strangers
Isn't either.
A longing for European
Hotel cafés and hands
Of children folded together
Like wings on a dove.

As she struggles home through
Splintered bridges and naked alleyways
She does not turn her head,
A tear falls from her eye
While she stares straight
Ahead without blinking.

She will not let her cries
Drown out imaginary laughter
And distant friends.
There is still magic in dreams
Even in laughable tragedies
Such as hers, there is magic.

She'll continue to make her
Footsteps on this earth
Even if there's no prints left
On them.
Through distant emotions
And paper triangle yearly reviews
She will look past tragedy and
Laugh at this human comedy
Just as so many have laughed at her.

Tears for Candy
(The Death of the American Dream Part II)

To her, intercourse is sad
With men of distinction.
But the hills of Hollywood
Blew visions of happiness
And higher places across
The lone Indiana plains
Where extinction and
Dreams are interchangeable.

How could one get lost
In such a beautiful place?
So she scraped up enough
Dough for a bus ticket
And said goodbye to
Oblivious backseat lovers
And worried parents as
She made her way to
Los Angeles as so many
Youngsters often do.

Upon arrival she is greeted by
A sad scene of painted vampires
Handing out flyers among
Smiling morticians with
Bawdy bandanas
Offering amphetamines and
A couch to wayward Hollywood
Transplants recently deposited
From the train station.

Careening through mad city thickets
Littered with discarded food containers
And copies of the LA Weekly that
Drift through the yellow breeze,
She fatally assumed that she
Would become discovered or

Make some important connections.

I have drank too many times
Among these carnivorous
Hollering streets and seen
The nightmare logic reflected
In the eyes of the dying and lost,
But to her this seemed like
A paradise a world away from
The moonshine backyard tractor
Parties and corner stores of
Her midtown youth.

She followed the walking cadavers
Dressed in leather pants and Converse
Shoes that ducked and darted
Between the beaming traffic lights
And cement landscapes
Wondering if glamour really
Existed among the bright billboards
And buzzing freeways.

Helicopters, cop cars, tattooed parasites
Carelessly passing by this liberated virgin
Obscenely unaware that sex
Sells in disowned alleyways
And rent by the hour heroin hostels.

Within a week's time, a Sunday
I believe it was, she picked
Up a copy of the LA Weekly
And scoured over the classifieds
As she took in the
Surrealist spectacle of
Zombies, junkies, whores
And protesting plastic musicians.
Her eyes stopped as she read
The thick black promising words:
Dancers Needed, No Experience Necessary.

Little did she know that within
Her beauty lay her mortality
Where vultures feed on
The sweet wine of innocence.
Her audition went well and
Within a week she had a gig,
Within a month she had a
Small apartment and an
Addiction as big as a battlefield.

She now dances among the
Mirrored walls reflecting
A gold pole of humiliation
That slides into a world
Of money-losing nothingness.
A paradise for lonely spurious
Unshaven men in suits who
Lurk in the shadows of red
Leather booths and small
Black square tables.

Withering away while discovering
Black market America, a new
Symbolic Western frontier
Void of heroes or gunslingers,
Only bald burly bouncers
And industrialist DJ's handing
Out grams of tweek for a
Smile and a dance.

The renaissance of wonder that
She hoped would await her
Has dismally fallen like a
Drunk in a rowboat.
"Look homeward," her inner voice
Calls out, but she knows all
Too well that she has dug a hole
She'll never crawl out of.
In this neon nightmare there will be

No more smells of breakfast
Drifting over paper thump porches.

Small town America now seems
Like a dream, a great divide
That she will never cross.
Her jellybean breasts bounce
To the soulless rhythm of
Haunted trumpeters as her
Licorice stick lips attempt
To feign happiness as dollar
Bills fall like leaves
In an autumn wind.

As the song fades out to
Muddled applause and cat calls
She collects what's left of
Her dignity off the checkered
Dance floor and wonders
How she ever got so far
From home and thinks to herself,
Los Angeles is a beautiful place
If you don't mind dying everyday.

The Science of Numbers
(The Death of the American Dream Part III)

Numbers are a tricky business,
He knew this all too well
Sitting in classes listening
To math problems that might
As well have been spoken
Through a Greek megaphone.
Carbonized syllables on aged
Pages taunting that they
Would never be deciphered.

Numbers are tricky indeed,
Especially in this economy.
A pristine subterranean school
Nestled within guarded valleys
That seemed miles away from
The unhappy alienated graffiti
Covered streets of the inner city.
With numbers being what they were
Any skeleton or warm body
Would be admitted as long
As seats were filled and
Tuition was paid up front.

Standing among the indignant intellectuals
Wondering, *who is this bum that*
Has crept in off the streets?
Mother did not realize any of this
With freedom flashing in her eyes.
So what if credit cards were maxed out
And she had holes in her shoes?
She didn't see the truth behind
These avaricious administrators
Who needed numbers to
Keep up appearances.

As she slept under second-rate sheets

In her frayed gray sweat pants
She dreamt of opportunity for
Her dissipated son who
Was conceived in the backseat
Of a rusted Chevy with
Dice blinking thirteen
Hanging from the ignition key.

Taking the tangerine colored bus
In and out of the city everyday
With his oversized uniform
Donated by vainglorious alumni
Doing their good deeds for the year,
This not too brilliant kid
Stepped into the steep ravines
Of haughty academia
Where black hole blackboards
Would devour him like stars
In the Milky Way.
Roaming crowded halls nobody
Seemed to notice that
He was as fragile as
Those pages and numbers
He was made to unscramble
On a daily basis.

Numbers can be frightening,
Narrow-minded street scamps
Awaiting his return back home.
Backward baseball cap logic
And tattoo philosophy blowing
Smoke and inanely unstudied
Reasoning into his diffident mind.

Hollow humanity entertaining ideas
Of what a man should really be.
Birdbrained barrio associates
Calling him a pussy for
Trying to get an education

All the while feeding
Into his fear and loathing
Of literary games and
Brawny deans of discipline.
Over his first year his
Grades sunk like concrete treasure chests
And his referrals multiplied
Like the pimples on his unkempt face.
He thought, *perhaps numbers*
Are a way out.

He would soon find that his
Sensible approach would not work.
Teachers and deans
Passing the buck to keep
The administration satisfied
With trumped-up numbers of achievement.

His mother lost in the
Heart of working class America
Would sit in on classes with
Her immensely embarrassed son,
Trying anything to keep her
Dream alive of having
Her son rise above the proletarian
Masses she had been around all of her pensive life.

His father fled years ago,
A common carrier sperm donor
Gone as quickly as the sun
That rises over a shushing shore.
Her tears and determined calls
To teachers would not
Be enough to save her son,
Another faceless number
Sitting behind a desk of discontent.

Through corners of classrooms
He was slowly transforming

Into a cold-blooded tyrant
Who daydreamed of escape.
He thought that one
Who could not be accepted
Could always be feared
And respected, he had found
His ticket out, a way to
Make a name for himself
That nobody owned
Among the calcified landscapes
And hoodlums of his neighborhood.

Without looking back, he
Dug into his tattered green backpack
And grabbed a chipped pocket knife
Determined to disappear forever
From this strange institution.

It is possible to destroy creatively.
Walk naked down the hall,
Start a food fight, smoke
Dope in the dean's office.
But this young man who had
Been beaten by his mother's
Dream and sculpted by
The daily scrimmage for
Survival in his neighborhood
Wasn't so bright.

He walked into the principal's
Office without anyone noticing
He was truant from his third
Period class under the
False pretense of procuring
A signature for a document.
Slipping behind the principal
He plunged in the unsteady blade
And the deed was done.

Numbers can be intimidating,
Ravaged images of concrete
And bars greeted him along
With his new number and
An orange suit that he would
Now be known by.
His former name stripped down
And floating away in space.
Staring away in dumb wonder
At his new home, his flustered
Mind soundlessly exploded
Into sharp shooting nothingness.

Numbers can be unfair.
Hard-eyed innocents and
Throw-away children
Given a number by a hostile
Judge pruning freedom
And creating career criminals.

Five years for this
Child of sixteen, an
Eternity into adulthood.
A release date death sentence
Rang out through that wooden
Courtroom as his mother
Watched another American
Dream smashed like a discarded
Thermometer on a horrid
Sidewalk that could be
Any street in America.

Rosary Regrets
(The Death of the American Dream Part IV)

Tattletale rusted wombs
Tell furious stories of
Bad influence and an
Agony of frostbite cold.
Memories relived every time
She passes a church
Where titanic pangs
Of shame clutch at her conscience.

She was raised in a Catholic family
Where tinker toy trials of guilt
Would smite her sleepy childhood.
Notoriously nauseous before
Every confession, religious fanatics
Looking for easy prey among
The rows of knock-kneed children.

Her hypocritical father preaching
Every Sunday after Saturday
Nights spent swallowing blue pills
And guzzling Jack Daniels.
His scorching tongue
Decaying the hopes of his
Fragile daughter.

As she became older
She took to the football fields
Where team captains held
Succulent roses at homecoming
Games that smashed
Her morality like a sledgehammer.
Tame lungs inhaling smoke and
Deliverance, a deliberate escape
From years of oppression and
Deserted expectations she
Could no longer withstand.

A sensual arena under
Constant construction, trying
To fit in among the cockroaches
And small town heroes.
Changing clothes on the
Way to school, she would
Light a cigarette and
Disown her borrowed faith.
Lipstick drenched in profanity,
Mother's workbench mascara
Autographed on her wishful eyes.

She went from playing tiddlywinks
To screwing around with boys
In backseats.
Filthy fox eyes searched for
Her behind bleachers at dances.
Another small town Shirley Temple
Scandalously sucking lollipops.

Outrageous parties, drunkenly
Wandering around in the middle
Of the street wondering if
Real people actually existed.
She had become a manufactured
Phony, just like her parents
She so despised.
A parking meter between
Her legs collecting
Spiritual unemployment.

Back alley doctors swapping
Money for well-kept secrets,
Phantom children left in dumpsters
As daylight crawls into another
Night of misspent youth.
If she ever told you her
Name it would not matter
For there is a girl like

Her in every city.

Shot glass sermons from
Bartenders led her into
Adulthood where spiked
Bullets of false wisdom
Sloppily led her home
To a pillowcase and a
Guilt-ridden assassination
Of the soul.

Many years later the
Irony would haunt her.
The guilt imparted to her
As a child that she
Had tried to escape
From with a cliché invention
Would return with a hollering vengeance.

You see, memories don't die as
Easy as one might like.
Memories don't know how
To say good goodbye, they
Watch from stained glass windows
Casting stovepipe rays of judgment.
Ashamed of her own nakedness
A modern day Eve lamenting
Discarded children from her youth.
Gymnasium vampires have been
Replaced by middle-aged
Pinocchios who never made
It out of Pleasure Island.
Solitary drinks shared
By amputated saints
Sitting on a row of bar stools.

Society has published
Her sins, this once little girl
Trapped in a life of regret

That she cannot escape.
Her years of stolen freedom
A prison cell, an unsuccessful
Escape, a guilt-ridden conscious.
The religion she once fled from
Now mocks her memories
With screaming ghosts of
Aborted children.
Trapped forever in what were
Supposed to be her wonder years.

The Blue Collar
(The Death of the American Dream Part V)

You still look the same
In your casual attire
Greeting me with a weary smile
Passersby talking of old times
Growing up together getting heroically hammered.

Rapidly approaching forty
You speak of dreams
And job interviews
Bitterly reminded that
Skipping college wasn't
Such a good idea.

Glorified cracker stackers
In light denim button-down shirts
Handing down orders to fire
Your friends you've
Worked with for so many years.

I imagine you at home
Mindlessly playing Madden
Opening up a corkscrew noose,
A pitiable escape from
The ten hour work days
That have bent your back
And sullied your ambitions.

The question remains and haunts.
Do you quit your usual habitations
To pursue your dream
Of guitar hero glories
On lighted stage above adoring fans
Or continue to
Work in retail
Where the pay is not so
Bad after twenty years

Of hard work and dedication?

But the burdensome truth
Remains that you're just
As disposable now
As you were when you first started.

Yet the conundrum continually taunts.
Do you keep slaving away
Hoping to save up enough
Money to achieve the
American dream and buy
A house or do you
Venture outside of
Simulated safety to
Chase your own desires?

Does happiness really consist
Of downing twelve beers every night
To forget smoldering sorrows
That should be left at work?
Did you let them turn your
Once bright aspirations
Into cynical opaque eyes?
Does owning a home really
Constitute freedom, or
Will it only serve as
Another watering hole
To drown out the days' sorrows?

Leave the past behind,
Forget the cruel tongue
That hung insults on you
Like tapestries on a windowless wall.
Forget the cement well poverty
Of your past.
Realize that you have overcome
The obstacles that drugged
And raped your mind of cobbled candor.

Take back your dreams and
Abandon green sleeping pill bottles of ale,
For it's not too late
To cut the noose America
Has made for you.
Cut the one size fits
All cookie cutter rope.
Defile that deadliest of dreams,
Come down from the dying tree
You've been perched on for so long.
Come down and feel
What it's like to live again.

America has no care
For the middle-aged
Blue collar working man.
History has shown many times
That you're as dispensable
As the plastic cup you
Fill with your jaded gin liquid escape.
Do not hope for
The death of a salesman.
Do not let your coffin
Be lined with sales figures
And distorted labor reports.
Crush the cancerous name tag.
Your life awaits you, my friend.
But as you well know
Dying is an art
And in another twenty
Years you will have perfected it.
Enough!
　　　　Enough!
　　　　　　　Enough!
Vanish the paperweight grave
And remember that
Only cats have nine lives.

The Lachrymist
(Epilogue to The Death of the American Dream)

Ceremonious crying for those
Crushed by this filament they
Call "The American Dream."
Our once great nation
Left in a state of somnolence
Deterred by defeat,
An austere expression
Chiseled on the masses.

An alacritous desire
To believe in a grand idea
Morose and endlessly brutal
Like our ocherous skyline.

Cry for the forgotten American.
Cry for Gatsby floating lifeless in a stagnant pool.
Cry for Loman and his corroding briefcase.
Cry for our pin stitched flag
Purchased through backbreaking
Slave labor.
Cry for Plath with head in oven
While Ted Hughes writes *Birthday Letters*.
Cry for Kesey and his rusted bus
Anchored by conformity and lost ideals.
Cry for the cobwebbed woman
Alone and facing middle age.
Cry for small town dreams
Devoured by ruinous poverty.
Cry for Morrison exiled
And alone in Père Lachaise without
Any bottle for solace.
Cry for the child with
The starving mind
Sitting in the back of the classroom.
Cry for the emerald hearted girl
Whose hopes fade under the

Crushing window of time.
Cry for our coal fire skies
That choke the old
And behead the daisies.
Cry for our recyclable
Heroes sent to war
Returned stripped of humanity.
Cry for Bukowski and
His disfigured face
Failing his father for a blade of grass.
Cry for Ann Sexton wandering
Down *Mercy Street*
In mother's old fur coat.
Cry for the addict nourishing
Veins with incense, death
And hours of desolation.
Cry for the crucifix
Smoldering in the fanatic's fire.
Cry for the housewife trapped
In her two story tombstone.
Cry for false freedom
Constantly shoved down
Mouths like communion wafers.
Cry,
        Cry,
                Cry.

Wake up America and take back
Your precious oxygen and
Sunken hopes promised
Through counterfeit constitutions.
Cry for God's sake!
Erase the ridiculous calm
And get angry!

Crying as therapy
Believing that only through
Pain, both physical and emotional,
Can one grow and

Move on to a
Higher level of being.
Cry…
Cry America for
Your tears are
Not wasted.

Lachrymology, a new
Philosophy to wake
Us from our collective slumbers
And inherit the dream
That is so rightfully ours.

Cry for the
Forgotten and aborted child
Who never had a chance.
Cry for our politicians
Whose failures become
Our washed out realities.
Show me the way
Pave me with shit…
America,
I've caught your delirium.

The Mountain Bears a Tear

Dead
      Girl
            Left
On a
Mountain
Path
Stolen
From
Home
No
Pillow
Or
Bed
On
This
Mountain
Gravesite.

Devil for Hire

Tormented transfiguration
Of the mind,
Temporarily authoritative entering
Like a magician.

I will perform the silent ceremony
Filling your heart with
Curious tall tale lies.
Monastery flowers wilting for
The priest as he passes.
Continuous, endless and nonsensical
Are the pleasant hallucinations
I'll use to blind your eyes
And bind your feet.

A question of faith,
The doubting face of the spouse,
The lying tongue of the child
All ambiguous scraps of my invention.
Your puerile wisdom combined
With my hate,
Intersecting like serpents on the staff of Hermes
Will destroy temples and their
Worshipers driven to their
Knees in conceived terror.

Mankind's end is my beginning.
My birth obsolete, a black
Cancer consciousness holding
Pregnant tombstones for
The dying bride and
Her rotten womb of despair.

I'm the voice behind every stool pigeon.
The prick of guilt born out of
The confusion of God
Leaving countries pleading for

Freedom, a negativist in
The truest sense of the word.

I'll perform my decadent lobotomy
Infiltrating the bourgeoisie.
My medieval hands alive and
Well controlling Wall Street
Plotting your downfall,
All routine in a day's work.
You wake up choking on
My final deposition that you'll
Take responsibility for.
The carcass of the kidnapped child,
The lost pet wandering and helpless,
The creator of discord and
Disaster stolen from God's mind.

Vomit out the feeling of acceptance
For my mushroom cloud liberation.
The underground mystic,
A fallen genesis,
An unfertile diseased
Dope fiend dictatorship,
The invisible scar on the mind
Etched on veins beneath the skin.

I don't need to scream through
The shadows any longer.
I've got you shaking and
Scratching beyond repair.
Confess your sins
That reveal your fractured
Integrity like an X-ray.

Another corpse, a conscious
Euthanasia of society.
Your ruin,
My next destination.
Eat your own filth through

My unwholesome advertising,
For my footprints
Are running your nations.
Devils rocking your infants' cradles
Editing emotions through
Dictatorship economics,
The reincarnation of death.
A divine intrusion weaving
My way through the
Unconscious streets of America.

Where the Wounded Things Are

Artificial karma emotionally wounded
Through vanity and imagined acceptances.
An intolerable radiance
Bankrupt and gray,
Obscure languages spoken
Through vacant skulls
That bid adieux to
Our materialistic world.

Keats, Tennyson, Shelley, Coleridge
Take refuge in the untouched nature
Away from the
Industrialization of our
Once pristine world.
Harmonious and incorruptible
The Romantics seeking
A return to Mother Earth
As she's tied down
And raped by progress.

Frankenstein's creation could
Find a home in this 21st
Century ravaged America
That our soiled reveries
And ambitions so impulsively
Created out of
Contempt and irrelevance.
For we no longer banish
The horrid and ugly,
Accepting the soulless
Red carpet heroes
Of our time.

Crumbs of a Dream

Birthplace
        unknowable
              flowers
                      recalled
                      faint
                      twilight
              girl
        throwing
        me
        backwards
  into
  a
clear water~~~~~~~~~~
grave.

The Glutton and the Libertine

Wilmot's ghost with pancake makeup
To mask his sexual shame
Presiding over a rainy Paris cemetery
Paying homage to Morrison
Who still wanders
Streets wrenched from the grave
By tourists on a crooked pilgrimage.

Fitzgerald's spirit searching
Heartbroken looking for
The ashes of Zelda
Among the ruins of a sanitarium.
Cobain, still not alone in
Seattle peering down
At his bench from that
Solitary window where
He wrote his last
Goodbye with
Pen and shotgun.

Thompson collecting cannonball ashes
Roaming his ranch with a bottle of pills.
Joplin, still clinging to her
Bottle of Southern Comfort
Wondering if she was ever pretty enough.

More,
      More,
            More,
Cries the public.
Your tragedies are our victories,
Our fables and legends.
Raping the dead and famous
One corpse at a time.
Vicariously experiencing fame
Through needles and fretboards.

Elaborate rituals of worship
Through torn posters and movies.
America only loves the famous
When they're dead,
Ravenously feeding on created
Myths and sold out stories
That begets this
Impulsively pillaged
Neon lit spiritually truant kingdom
Of dead stars
And stolen stripes.

21st Century Eve

Gentle doves know not
The quibble of derelicts
Crowing out obscenities
And complaints among
Passersby on a lone midnight street.

Absinthe armies of
Graveyard virgins sacrificed
On a green altar of squander.
Brides of Satan fumbling their
Passports to heaven in
Hazardous shaking hands.

Vain girls keeping vampire hours,
Sunset alarm clocks
And distracted mirrors
Of vanishing beauty
Stolen and corrupted
By media images
That scar the school girl
And seduce the slut.

The imaginary "American Dream"
Driving a knife
Into the crux of our youth
With changing promises of
Marked freedom that
Makes the mother grimace
And cracks the ancient father's heart.

IV
Order the Deceased to March
I dare not wake until Heaven sends its deadliest angel

Moonrise Country

Dying shadows set with the sun,
White bone stars
Can see no color.
The dope fiend rises
Sickened and bruised.
Flowers topple, dissipating
Genius, trading secrets
For blank tapestries.

Tongues speaking gibberish,
A hostile misinterpretation.
Crows for currency,
Dead space for rent,
Wasted flesh never resting.
Nightmares merge with gravestones
In the deteriorating distance.

The lone wolf gazes
With intensity at altars
Burning in midnight's eternal frost.
Tangled and disordered
Emotions in an unpopulated suburb.
The child cries from the grave
Clutching rodents suddenly
Streaming from the dirt.

Withering thickets hunched
Over earth's bedrock.
Let no mortal tread
Upon this dwarfed eyesore acropolis
Where debauched masters of
The moonlight circle under
Abandoned outlandish clouds.
Mad Oedipus holds
The knife, itching for
Mother's brooch pin flesh.

There is no wind,
    In this
        Insane
Cowboy landscape,
Fevered and claw cut
Stilled and shivering.
Grandmother froze here
Sipping brandy out of straws
Woven in a human patchwork
A
    Country
        That
           Even God
                Won't visit.
An extended holiday to Hell.

Some Kind of Glory

Why dig up the corpse
To revive old memories?
Photos will do just as
Fine to fill the
Spaces of a lonesome mind,
Cast away pride through
Streams of virtuous tears.
Your memory, my epitaph
Your love, my decay
Strained rhetoric reciting prayers
Over your painted tomb.

Your ghost, my imaginary counterpart
That dignifies my sorrows
Within a smog smeared sunset.
Unlettered hymns
Familiar and forsaken
As the wretched windblown
Hills of the city of angels.

Awaiting Autumn

Old mirrors carve deep diverging lines
In the autumn twilight of her face.
Strange old men stand behind
Cracked lipstick containers.
A river of phantom lovers
To haunt her memories
Beaten by the waves of time
    She
        Sleeps
            Among
                The
Disordered
And numbered stars
    Of
        Night.

Hemlock on the Rocks

Craving veins awake
A ferocious appetite
Kindled like branches.
Bolt the doors
Before I seek my rueful sacrifice
On a burning bar stool
Where venom flows freely
And turns this addict
Into a sharp tongued troll.

An accidental ritual
Born out of adolescent carelessness
And baggage, booze and basins
Where I vomit out saintly freedom.
Compelled to destroy
With every sip,
A heroic rumpus
That would make
Even Bukowski blush.

Unloading years of private invisible luggage
On strangers, statues and city streets.
No debt to society
Will be paid tonight…
I have an open tab.

Saturday Night at Z's

Pissing off a cracked wooden porch
Smoking cigarettes and slamming vodka
While REO Speedwagon blares
Through the sliding door.

Dancing drunkards badly singing
And changing lyrics among
Fierce political debates
And bouncing quarters.
Jägermeister jump-start at
2 A.M., clumsily playing pool
Now pissing on the stairs
That lead up to the
Dilapidated porch
Stargazing and drunk dialing.

Passing out with the rising sun,
Fumbling for blankets
Walking over a human
Carpet looking for
A place to crash
As bluebirds look
Down in shame
On the ruins
Exiting the American night
With no music to follow.

A Prolonged Absence

I abandoned my craft
For the bastard orphan bottle
That kissed me with liar's lips.
Soddenly kissing the moon's celestial glow
Squandering creativity for
Mangled nerve endings
Green glass assassins
Leaving me parched in a gutter.

A grandiose colossus downfall,
A great preposterous idiot
Falling and wandering
Alone, amused, abused
Ambushed and absent
From reality and responsibility.

A decade of debauchery
Spinning in midnight's streets
Pissing on the steps of churches
Hiding out in the attics of bars.
Endow the drunk with
Absolute power and
Watch the destruction
Of a great mind
Fiery enough to feel
But not quite clear on meaning.

Ghosts and priests side by side
Passing judgment from
An eighty proof pool inferno.
Perhaps I've quit Heaven
The night is my haunt.
I could spawn ridiculous fables
From those tormented years,
I could atone for my collapsed condition,
But I need not ask for penance.
I've rekindled an old spark

And found salvation in the pen.

American Stonehenge

The passive rambling of the solitary drunk
Speaking his promise with every breath
To those who will lend an ear
To his rare broadcast.
Bar stool philosophy breaking
The piano keys
Hanging in the stagnant air
Of stale cigarettes
And cheap divine mead.

A grand museum of human decay
And perishable dreams
That sprout beneath
A chipped slogan imprinted mirror.

Here you will find no books
Nor priceless works of art.
There is only bone which
Casts haphazard shadows
Of debased delusions drenched
In alcohol held by
Grand tragedians who
Somehow never made
It to the next
Stage of existence.

This is where pity thrives
In afternoon shot glasses
Riding on cider carousels.
Bottles stacked resembling
A small sullen Stonehenge
For drunken Druids
Who worship the abilities
Of bottled spirits.

Switching Tables

Twelve step sobriety snobs
Ruining my writing environment.
I'll buy them each a beer
If they'll leave.
You were much quieter
When you used to drink.

Casual Friday businessman
Holding a banana and
The attention of a sultry co-worker.
I'll pay for your hotel room
If I can have my table back.

Plain Jane in jogging shoes
Occupying a velvet couch
While a balding buzz cut
Pseudo-intellectual casts
Intruding glances from
Behind his laptop.

Colliding conversations meeting
Mid-air pouring down white noise
As I look for a place to write.
No room at the inn
For this American poet
Clutching on to Plath
And a half-filled moleskine.

Hammered on Henley Street

How the precious glass
Will waste the wrinkled minutes.
You shall find foaming sepulchers
Of amber influence
Born of advanced ignorance.

Mend the broken heart with
Sweet stinging graces of
Sickly stirring spirits.
My muse does
Invent my soundless death.

Empty Pot, No Rainbow

Hallucinating leprechauns
Through puzzling passages
Of green alien ale.

A toxic cocktail
Burning like Halley's Comet
In my rotgut stomach.

The Irish don't
Need a holiday to drink
And I don't need an A.A. meeting
To justify my sorrows
Swerving mad
And sluggish
Behind the wheel.

Dissolving waltzes of
Intoxication speeding
Down America's highways,
Converging streams of consciousness
Conflicting with spinning sirens
      Strayed
           Over
                The yellow
                    Line of
                        Authority
Losing
      Order
To save
Drunken relics
That roll around
The floor of the
Passenger seat.
A telling suicide
Racing inwards
Towards death.
502's aren't just for jeans.

Purrfect Guide

Syd Barrett's cat
Wandering alone
Slinking across painted floorboards.
Falling asleep on a sheet of acid.

A true and original Cheshire cat
Unable to point direction
Saying, "Wear my eyes
To see no thought."
Abstract lines
On a spider web map
Twisting and turning
On a battered Cambridge street.

Swinging London

See Emily Play
Among ghosts at the UFO club.
Townshend, Hendrix and Barrett
Searching for *Gnomes* in the Gog Magog Hills.
Waters going into an *Interstellar Overdrive*
Setting the Controls for the
Heart of the Sun
While Syd fries an egg on stage
And *Arnold Layne* steals
Undergarments off of washing lines.
The *Vegetable Man Screams*
His last Scream
Before *The Piper at*
The Gates of Dawn
Leaps over to
The Dark Side of the Moon.

Passion's Folly

Her pleading eloquence conjures
Visions of knighthood and princely thrones
That cannot be wiped away.
Doting desires, my lust becomes a prison
Where I'm exiled from emotion
Through my own misdeeds.

Saintly sin taught me the way
Leading me into
A secluded chamber
Showing me the key
And walking away without goodbye.

My tears create reflections of dishonor
Nobly revealed through memories
Of you and what was to be.

FWY

Declining stillness
I wish to remain in motion
And avoid the irony
Of what they call rush hour.
If everyone is in such a hurry
Then why is nobody moving?

Treasure Hunt

There is no X on the vagina
Yet millions of teenage
Boys try to solicit
Their way into
The pants of unsuspecting girls
Through bad poetry,
Cheap gas station bouquets
And premeditated primping.

Davy Jones' Locker
Is filled with these
Dumbfounded dorks looking for booty
Sentenced to a prison
Of internet porn
And tall tales
Swapped in locker rooms…
Try finding "The G-Spot" young lads
No map or GPS required.

Crimson Sorrow

The bloodstained hands
Of the virgin hunter
Can never be cleansed
Of the guilt from
Killing an innocent animal.

A most foul hauteur
Descends, uncoiled
Like wild locusts
Over the face of the
Man who slaughters
Not for food but
For gaudy sport.

Horrific images invade
Magazines gossiping of
Celebrities in fur coats,
Mounted prizes assaulting
Walls in restaurants and studies.

Celebrate the deer,
The fox and the moose!
Give them back their
Horns, claws and teeth.
Give the eagle back
His wings and talons
Fight on their terms,
Subjugate yourself
To their helplessness.

Such abuses scream of
Pride and hubris.
Camouflage cowards substituting
A gun for a penis
And attacking the innocent
While our forests burn with shame.

Nothing in Between

Pristine emeralds plucked
From nature's womb
Implanted lonely and mourning
On a ring of deceit
And black hole promises
That stray like shadows.

View From a Downtown Apartment

Carbon monoxide arriving
Through the mail slot.
Garbage can porch lights,
Spiteful and secretive neighbors
A row of mausoleum apartments
Dying in the snake orchid city.
Needles among the flowers
Shining in the distressed sunset.

The Pathological South

Boo Radley's ghost
Saving the children of midnight.
Noble Atticus entombed
In small town racism,
A Southern sarcophagus
Spread against a Confederate landscape
Where morphine mockingbirds
Perch atop Mrs. Dubose's window.

Victorian Blackness

Blue lines outline
The flame that
Burns in a vacant window.
Don't bother knocking…
Nobody's home.

What Love Is

Before we were engaged
I used to hold my farts in
And now that I'm married
I won't hold back.

Shitting with the door open
I'm live entertainment
Scratching my balls
Before breakfast
Bloated and bare-assed…
You don't need a robe
When you're married.

Heroin Withdrawals: The Torchlight Trilogy

Nightmare #1 (Cold Sweats, Dry Sheets)

Candle eye bats
Fly beneath a gothic moon.
Cold blackness, holy pews
Delicate saints from
A mystical church
Call out over the
Sound of a distant trumpet
That separates the eye of God
From faces in the darkness.

Nightmare #2 (In Methadone Minor)

Borrowed room with
A mahogany stare,
Frosting decorated ceiling
Dripping down drowned faces
That cling to the bedside
While I push the button
Screaming for security
Waking up holding
Gun and empty soul.

Nightmare #3 (Praying For Relapse)

Driftwood dolls peering through keyholes,
Nervous and cross-legged
Ten days dead
Twitching and crawling walls.
Photographs laughing over
Creaking porches,
Clock hand shadows
Painting inaccessible doors
No room to escape.
Shrieks proceed abstractions
Departing to deprivation,

Myself alone
And trembling.

Paging Dr. Bendo

Banished from the court of Charles II
Drunkenly and mistakenly handing Charles
The wrong poem criticizing the King
For his obsession with sex over
That of his kingdom or
Was it his late-night scuffle
With the night watchman that
Led to his banishment and
Created this legendary doctor?

Setting up a sulfurous stall
On Tower Hill this exiled
And invented depraved physician
And surreptitious sperm donor
Claiming to cure "barrenness"
And various gynecological disorders
Put down his powerful pen
In exchange for his
Infectious penis percolating
Disease through digestible
Syllables of sin.

Flickering genius, this divine rake
Not afraid to criticize or satire
The hypocrisy of his country.
A fifteen year drunken rampage
With his Merry Gang.
Lampooning Charles' supposed
Motives in pushing religious tolerance
Through *Sodom*, this princely
Devil of debauchery
Turning Charles into Bolloxinion
And his queen into Cuntigratia.
Wilmot, the original rock star
Influencing Aphra Behn
The architect of women's rights.

Look not to the hippies
And 60's idealists as
True innovators of sexual
Freedom and women's rights.
Look to the Restoration Era poets of England
For planting the seeds
That would grow to
Awaken a dead-eyed America
Out of its lightning struck illusions
Of stability and nuclear families
Living in shimmering sanctuaries of solace.

The PMRC advocating censorship,
Washington housewives
Crudely constructed Frankenchrists
Dictating morals and commandments
Carved not of stone,
But out of ignorance.
Waist-deep in history yet unaware of
17th century British literature and
The Disabled Debauchee,
Signor Dildo, A Ramble in St. James Park,
The Imperfect Enjoyment and
The Disappointment.

Lysander prematurely ejaculating
Onto the pages of history
That 20th century censors
Refuse to remember or read.
Adhering to Puritanical practices
While our first amendment
Freedoms go up in flames.

Writer's Remorse

Ungodly landscapes,
Forest funerals,
Chainsaw symphonies
Of annihilation.
The tree shrieks
Covered in grease
And gasoline.
Somber clouds crying
Tears of disapproval.

A global abortion
Effortlessly emptied
And set afire
By man and politicians
Who hide behind
The pseudonyms of corporations.

Motherly blood spilt
Flowing into mouths
Of corpses,
Teeth extracted for gold.
Even the dead are for sale
As modern day
Pirates pillage land
Over the cicatrix of America.

This 21st century holocaust
Masked by the bastard lover progress.
Branches carried away by gin poles
And cranes in burlap death-gowns.

Even the writer is
Not completely free of
Guilt as he pours ink
Over the cadavers of tortured timber
While editing old memories
In the hopes of becoming brilliant.

Education (Temporarily Under Construction)

Walk into any American classroom
You can observe indifferent adolescents
Carelessly sleeping on textbooks
Intellectually starving from
Educational malnourishment
Deficient in knowledge
A mental scurvy of the mind.

Teachers with loosened ties
Reading newspapers with
Legs propped on desks.
Spitballs, zip tying backpacks
Anarchy in the classroom
As the children rebel
Though not really sure
Against which cause.
What is left for
These martyrs of the apocalypse
With broken homes, bongs
And bad haircuts?

Ecstasy sold in bathroom stalls,
Texting during lectures,
Failing before they've even started.
Writing more on bathroom walls
Then they do in their notebooks.
Crudely laced Converse paving
The way to the unemployment line
While lazy tenured teachers
Continue to pass these kids
On to the next stage
Of the American nightmare.

Ouroboros

Wedding vows recited beneath
A hostile sun.
Sweat beads pouring down
Bride and groom.
Promises to hold and cherish
Promises to love in times of
Sickness and in health
Promises to remain
Together until death.
Promises…
Ambassadors of good intention
Paving the way
To hell and heartbreak.
Golden rings placed
On sweetbread appendages,
Backs stiffen and a kiss
Is exchanged among
Tears and small smiles of approval.

Hold your applause, save your
Tissues for a later date,
For no ring can
Contain an appetite
For carnal knowledge
Or a wandering eye
That thinks of someone else.
Deep-rooted desires of the flesh
Already spreading like ivy on a fence
Over these recently blessed rings.

Save your tears for
The sleepdrunk nights of abuse.
Save your tears for
The endless neon glitter
Of the city bars
Where women with
Blackberry stem legs

Call from quiet corners
Oozing seduction from
Candlelit crotches
And red silk encased tongues
Luring husbands whose
Chastity withers before
Their pithless hands
That destroy families
And give birth to the widow.

The Familiar Stranger

A smile forged
Out of concentration
Is nothing more
Than a subtle "Fuck You."

Do not return such vulgar gestures.
Leave them gratified
By your sudden exit
For they never really
Cared how you were doing
To begin with.

It's quite curious indeed
How one can be
Absent yet present
At the same time.

Hollow handshakes,
Well planned out pats on the back,
Hugging with the
Sincerity of a mannequin
Our society has become
A group of self-absorbed passengers
On a paved plastic road
To nowhere in particular.

Fuck (The Yin &Yang)

It's the mother of all cuss words
Damned and detested by many.
Such foolish nativities spawned
By short-sighted students of censorship.

Where there is evil
There is also good.
For the world must remain
In harmonious balance.
Sorry mother, but
Fuck is really not
Such a terrible word.
It masks the fury of the enraged
But also falls into many grammatical categories.

Can it be used as an infix?
Absofuckinglutely!
Can it be used as a verb?
You bet, haven't you
Ever been fucked by Ticketmaster
And their ridiculous service fees?
Can it be used as a noun?
Ask the fucker who stole your parking space.

Can it be a term of affection?
You're one smart fucker
If you answered yes.
Can it be used as an adverb?
Haven't you ever met someone
Who talks too fucking much?
Can it be used as an adjective?
It certainly can if you've
Ever had a job where you
Did all the fucking work, but got
No credit for it.

It comes in handy in math,

Especially when you don't
Understand the fucking questions
On your algebra homework.

If you think about it,
It's not any worse than damn.
What if Rhett Butler's last
Words to Scarlett O'Hara
In *Gone With the Wind*
Had been "Frankly, my dear, I don't give a fuck?"
It really wouldn't have made much of a difference.

It can be used as an inquiry,
Such as who wrote this
Fucking poem?
And, most importantly, it can be
Used to describe incompetence,
Like all those dim-witted
Fuckers who condemn this great word.

Sure, it can be a vulgar
Term for a beautiful act of love.
It can be used as a terrible
Insult or slur, but the
Educated person knows that it's
Just a fucking word.

Heroin(e)

Heroin notebook epidemics,
Everyone wants to be a
Psychopathic junkie and
Write memoirs.
Everyone wants to die,
But only if a camera is around.
Dead soul adolescents,
Reality prophets, strung out
And fighting on MTV.
Crying for mother
Once the director says "Cut!"

Smuggled identities for an
Episodic curiosity examining
The behavior of the volunteering dead.
Change the channel
And send these bastards
Back home ashamed
And insecure.

Lacking Matter

Fragile glass acquaintances
Gracious invisible people
That I never really knew.
Tongue-tied over drinks
And televised sporting events.
A common monument for pretentiousness.

Such virtue breathes
Life into every bar
And casual handshake.
Painting rhetoric through
Intoxicated insincerity
And counterfeit emotion.

In the end we are
Only left with our
Character and skeletons
Blackmailing Jesus to
Find out who
Our friends really were.

The Dying Tree

Swing,
     Swing,
          Swing,
Swing from the tree,
Swing you mindless fools
And cowards of conformity.
Swing from the societal rope
That's been cast around
Your neck since birth.

Swing, you who believes
Whatever the news tells you.
Swing, you enslaved addict
Whose life depends on desultory resolutions.
Swing, you politicians
Who smile behind lies.
Deathly guests who invade our homes through
Teleprompter promises shot through
A transmission beam exorcised of reason.
Swing, you fundamentalists
Who distort religion with lying lizard tongues.
Swing, you who turn the other way
Ignoring the homeless man's vacant hand.
Swing, you censors of free speech
Born with closed eyes
Thinking you could see.
Swing, you reality TV rejects
Who put fame above dignity,
Daily drunkards lost in a television constellation.
Swing, you street thugs
Local trolls who use the innocent for kindling.
Swing, you pedophile priest
Hiding behind a cardboard morality collar.
Swing, you adolescent
Giving up through drug-addicted departure
Before your life has even begun.
Swing, you fad follower

Who believes in good health
But doesn't read labels
And substitutes plastic surgery for exercise.
Swing, abusers of animals
So-called armor plated superior
Beings with no conscience or pity.

Swing from the tree
Bandaged by bullet holes,
Handcuffs and guilty nostalgia.
Branches lifting a valedictory salute
Farewell to dreams,
Farewell to thought,
Farewell to life.

Come back down
And live again America.
Cut the patriotic umbilical cord
That becomes your noose.
Realize that bipartisanship
Ends at our borders
And that we are all the same.
Abandon the sterile seeds
That give birth to
Rotting branches.
Come down awakened and anew.
Realize that you are human
Standing on the edge
Of the final frontier.
Tomorrow is untouchable
Carpe Diem!
Your dreams begin
As the stars blink
Hello to the dawn.

John Golden is a writer and a hopeless Rock 'n' Roll addict who currently resides in Long Beach, California. He has been writing since kindergarten when he used to dictate poems to his mother. When he's not writing or teaching he can be found contemplating the moon and all things nocturnal.

This is John Golden's second book of poetry. He is currently at work writing his first short story collection, *The 75 Club*.

Photograph by Dennis Zanabria
Long Beach, California

CONTENTS, COMETS, CONQUESTS

IV. Order the Deceased To March

www.ingramcontent.com/pod-product-compliance
Lightning Source LLC
Chambersburg PA
CBHW062221080426
42734CB00010B/1982